Chamber Music
The Poetry of Jan Zwicky

Chamber Music
The Poetry of Jan Zwicky

Selected
with an
introduction by
Darren Bifford and Warren Heiti
and an interview with
Jan Zwicky

LAURIER POETRY SERIES

WILFRID LAURIER
UNIVERSITY PRESS

Wilfrid Laurier University Press acknowledges the support of the Canada Council for the Arts for our publishing program. We acknowledge the financial support of the Government of Canada through the Canada Book Fund for our publishing activities.

Library and Archives Canada Cataloguing in Publication

Zwicky, Jan, 1955–
[Poems. Selections]
   Chamber music : the poetry of Jan Zwicky / selected with an introduction by Darren Bifford and Warren Heiti.

(Laurier poetry series)
Includes bibliographical references.
Issued in print and electronic formats.
ISBN 978-1-77112-091-3 (pbk.). — ISBN 978-1-77112-092-0 (pdf). —
ISBN 978-1-77112-108-8 (epub)

   I. Bifford, Darren J. (Darren John), 1977–, editor   II. Heiti, Warren, 1979–, editor   III. Title.
IV. Series: Laurier poetry series

PS8599.W53A6 2015   C811'.54   C2014-905281-2
                                                 C2014-905282-0

Front-cover image by Robert V. Moody; labyrinth.zenfolio.com. Cover design and text design by Pam Woodland.

© 2015 Wilfrid Laurier University Press
Waterloo, Ontario, Canada
www.wlupress.wlu.ca

This book is printed on FSC recycled paper and is certified Ecologo. It is made from 100% post-consumer fibre, processed chlorine free, and manufactured using biogas energy.

Printed in Canada

Table of Contents

Foreword

The Laurier Poetry Series began in 2004 with the appearance of *Before the First Word,* a volume of Lorna Crozier's poetry most ably edited by Winnipeg poet Catherine Hunter. Our hope was to bring contemporary Canadian poetry to its readers in a different way — by selecting thirty-five poems from across a poet's career, and by asking the editor and the poet to write an engaging and accessible introduction and afterword, respectively. Crozier and Hunter set the bar very high.

I admit that one ambition I had in mind then — I still do — was to match the reach of the New Canadian Library. I imagined, hoped that what that series has done, mostly for Canadian fiction, the Laurier series would do for Canadian poetry. I hoped that in the high school and university classroom, poets would be better served by a volume that represented their work more widely than the usual anthology, with one or at best a few poems from each poet. And I hoped that more readers, old and new, beyond the classroom, maybe outside of Canada, would find these volumes appealing.

Ten years later, with the twentieth volume just gone to press — and with the very recent and happy experience of using ten of the Laurier volumes, including Crozier's, in a fourth-year university class on contemporary Canadian poetry — a warm and vivid image arises in memory of poet Brian Henderson, then as now the Director of Wilfrid Laurier University Press, asking me over a beer on a hot June afternoon in 2002 in Toronto, at the Learneds, whether I might be interested in editing a series like this one. Then as now, I thought the idea was excellent. I didn't know if it would fly, though Brian's was, then as now, an inspired idea. A few more beers and an hour or so later, we agreed to give it a shot.

Over this last (fast!) decade the dedicated group that Brian leads at WLUP — especially managing editor Rob Kohlmeier and his luminous team — have worked with an unimaginably wide range of poets and poetics. To what little I knew in 2004 about publishing, they have added their consummate and patient professionalism.

What continues to inspire me about the Laurier Poetry Series, or LPS, has been its reception across the country. The love and art and passion and intimacy that twenty editors and twenty poets have brought to their volumes; the innumerable hours and conversations and meetings, the thousands of emails between and among poets and editors and Wilfrid Laurier; the generous reviews in the country's journals; the reception in classrooms and beyond: all of this eloquently speaks to the joyful proliferation of poetry in Canada today — and tomorrow. What a tremendous wealth of poets and readers we have here! What vital riches!

With each new volume, the Laurier Poetry Series hopes to continue to recognize the growing provenance of this wealth, the wide range of these riches. Our poets — and their readers — deserve nothing less.

— *Neil Besner*
General Editor

Biographical Note

Jan Zwicky has published nine collections of poetry, including *Songs for Relinquishing the Earth* (1996), which won the Governor General's Award, *Robinson's Crossing* (2004), which won the Dorothy Livesay Prize, and most recently *Forge* (2011), which was short-listed for the Griffin Prize. Her books of philosophy include *Wisdom & Metaphor* (2003) and *Lyric Philosophy* (1992), recently reissued by Brush Education, and *Alkibiades' Love*, a collection of essays, which is forthcoming with McGill-Queen's University Press. Zwicky grew up on the Prairies, was educated at the Universities of Calgary and Toronto, and currently lives on the West Coast of Canada.

Introduction

> *Within the discipline of criticism, nothing is more difficult than praise. To speak of what you love — not admire, not know to be good, not find reasonably interesting, not feel briefly moved by or charmed by — to speak of such work is difficult because the natural correlatives of awe and reverence are not verbal.* — Louise Glück

In the first lines of "Cashion Bridge," Jan Zwicky writes, "It would be as well at the outset to admit / how even to have said this much / is to have failed." Ineffability has always been at the centre of Zwicky's work. Lyric poetry's relationship to the ineffable is especially paradoxical: using words, such poetry attempts to point at what is wordless. Zwicky writes, "Good poems — including poems like [Sue] Sinclair's 'Red Pepper,' which elaborates a single metaphorical insight — are notoriously difficult to teach: ask any poet or sensitive English professor.... One often has the sense with a good poem that everything that *can* be said *has* been said, and perfectly, in the poem itself." With this cautionary note in mind, we shall not attempt to teach Zwicky's poetry or paraphrase its meaning. Let us consider the etymology of the English word "introduction." The *Oxford English Dictionary* indicates that the word is derived from the Latin verb "*introducere*, from *intro-* the inside + *ducere* to lead." Compare the word "education," which is traceable to the same Latin root: "*educere* lead out." An introduction, then, is the reverse of an education. Instead of being led out under the sunlight, we are led back into the many-windowed chambers of the books. Roaming through these chambers, we have noticed some things: a tiger-lily; a golden, tattered leaf; a bone-white bell; a cat's-eyed slice of rock.

METAPHILOSOPHY. **Exhibit: "The Geology of Norway."** More than a few of Zwicky's poems are explicitly philosophical. Importantly, her poetry does not merely make reference to philosophers and their problems; it also makes a contribution to philosophy. The resources indigenous to poetry — its imagery and music — are *also* modes by which we might think truly about the world. In an earlier poem from *The New Room*, "Language Is Hands," we hear the emergence of a characteristic vocal register — one that later reaches a crescendo in central poems from *Songs for Relinquishing the Earth*. It is a voice in dialogue with the Western philosophical tradition; sometimes this dialogue is a quarrel, but a respectful one. A poem such as "Cashion Bridge," for example, might find a place in an advanced class on epistemology. Or consider "The Geology of Norway": this poem offers an account of Wittgenstein's philosophical development. The voice that speaks is that of the later Wittgenstein, having retreated to his hermitage in Norway and looking back on the failure but also the aspiration of his earlier work. What is the desire that animates his first book, the *Tractatus Logico-Philosophicus*?

"I have wanted there to be / no story," says the voice of the poem. I have wanted there to be no unfolding of events in time, the complicated flux of circumstances that gives rise to tragedy. "I have wanted / only facts." — And what is a fact? It is "a geologic epoch / rendered to a slice of rock you hold between / your finger and your thumb." Such a fact is an ahistorical spatial structure; it is determinately articulated, and it can be completely described with the diamond-like precision of the perfect word. To borrow the central metaphor of the *Tractatus*, a fact can be *pictured* by a proposition. But this theory of meaning assumes that the substratum of the world is motionless, changeless; that it will remain motionless while we analyze it. But "when meaning holds still long enough to get its picture taken, it is dead." — The Tractarian theory cannot make sense of the flow of magma, or the sound of wind in leaves, or the myriad non-linguistic gestures that animals make. Consider the refrain: "The hand moving is the hand thinking." What becomes of the Tractarian theory when all of these static, disconnected pictures — these snapshots of the world — are set in motion?

In her notes to *Wittgenstein Elegies* (which collects the "five older cousins" of "The Geology of Norway"), Zwicky refers to the "crucial incident" that helps to explain the transition from the Tractarian picture theory of meaning to the later theory of gestural meaning. The poem "In the Elder Days of Art" renders the incident as follows: "Gritty railroad din, the click, the rock / And shuffle. Silhouette against / A sooty window, open hand, palm up: 'Show me / the general form of proposition here, root / Common structure!'" The speaker is Piero Sraffa, a lecturer in economics at Cambridge. He is making a gesture of contempt, brushing the underneath of his chin with his fingertips, and challenging Wittgenstein to provide the logical picture which will capture the gesture's meaning. This dimension of meaning, rooted in and expressed through bodily movements, is more vast and primordial than the dimension of meaning encompassed by propositions. One of the links between Wittgenstein's earlier and later views, according to Zwicky, is "the conviction that linguistic meaning is merely one *facet* of a larger phenomenon, and not always a paradigmatic facet at that." This larger phenomenon is what Zwicky calls "lyric meaning": it "can underlie and inform linguistic meaning, but it is, at the same time, broader in scope. Its root is gestural."

LYRIC AND NARRATIVE. **Exhibits: "Your Body" and "Transparence."** At least as early as *The New Room*, we see instances of stories compressed and interjected into otherwise lyric poems. In *Songs for Relinquishing the Earth*, these interjections seem to become motivic, a kind of counterpoint to "the futureless unnarrative of light." Compare the first stanza from "Your Body" with the first two stanzas from "Transparence":

> Like that couple I heard about later
> who hit a snowy owl one night in a storm
>   out of nowhere, huge, impossible
>   velvet crunch jack-knifed back into the blizzard, good
>   god, stopped somehow, dry-throated, half-knowing, scared
> to look, ashamed not to
>   — so,
> it now seems to me, I arrived at the door of your room.

*

> I would reply to Pythagoras
> nor can the soul
> become pure light.
>
> Or if it does, the experience,
> unless you are freakishly lucky — like
> that woman, thrown from her car, her car
> rolling and bouncing up one side of the embankment and then
> back down, to land on top of her, except
> the roof had been dented by the guardrail
> and it came down with the hollow
> over her and she escaped
> unscathed — will kill you.

In both poems, a story is dropped into one pan of an analogy. Like that couple who hit a snowy owl, the speaker arrives at the door of her father's room; like that woman who miraculously escaped from a car accident, only a freakishly lucky person could survive the experience of becoming pure light. In both poems, the story works *as though* it were an image, one half of a metaphor — it has that kind of intensity, not unlike the density of an imploded star. And in both poems, the gravity of the story dents and bends the syntax.

But the eros of lyric thought is different, Zwicky has claimed, from that of sequential thought, and their structures are different. A lyric structure — such as an attuned violin — is resonantly integrated and polydimensional. By contrast, a sequential structure — such as a journalistic story (what one of our students has called "coffee-time news") or an analytic argument — is unidimensional. And yet: "In a lyric composition, moments of analysis can be set in lyric relation." Maybe we could say that this is an inspiration, for example, for some of Zwicky's hybrid poems: an attempt to show that pieces of narrative can be worked into the (lyric) pattern of the world, "as a fleck can be worked into a tweed."

HISTORY AND ANONYMITY. Zwicky's fifth book of poetry, *Robinson's Crossing*, is (among other things) a meditation on history. — What *is* history? A theory of past events, ordered sequentially? — If we approach these poems with that expectation, we shall be disoriented. Of the history poems in the book, we might distinguish between two sorts: those that reflect, lyrically, on the subject of history ("Nothing moves: the walker, / who is walking, does not move. / That's history for you...."); and those that are themselves historical — but in a special sense: they are personal histories. The angel of history which inhabits the former sort of poem is Walter Benjamin's *Angelus Novus*: "His face is turned toward the past. Where a chain of events appears before *us, he* sees one single catastrophe, which keeps piling wreckage upon wreckage and hurls it at his feet." Here history is envisioned as the oil sands or the clear-cut or the rhetoric of the technocrat. Against this background, one of the book's epigraphs, by Gaston Bachelard, is significant: if we humans must live in time, then each of us "should speak of his roads, his crossroads, his roadside benches; each of us should make a surveyor's map of his lost fields and meadows." Zwicky's personal historical poems offer such a surveyor's map. Collectively, they attempt to recognize "some track that's always been there, / rose-edged, trailing off at dusk down to the river"; or to construct a human order "that respects, acknowledges, or gives access to another order without destroying it (or some other). A path through the woods, a warm winter coat."

In calling these histories "personal," we do not mean pseudo-confessional poetry, "all those blood-and-guts / home truths, the stupid / gothic grab of land and family"; instead, let us think of something closer to Roo Borson's *Personal History*: essays that recall confession to its etymological (and spiritual) roots of *acknowledgement*. The speaker in Zwicky's poetry — not a stable entity for any poet — is reticent and usually uninterested in offering up the dregs of her memory. Unlike Robert Lowell's inward-looking confessional verse (for example), Zwicky's poetry does not find its source in "what really happened" for its own sake. The poet does a poor job if she looks to her poetry to magnify her personality, to make a myth of her life. Zwicky has written *against* the Romantic exaltation of the ego. Her poetry has an opposite orientation and a contrary desire. In this respect its spirit is not unlike that of classical Chinese Mountains and Rivers poetry: a spirit that aims to make the self transparent to the world.

 Exhibit: "Robinson's Crossing." This poem belongs to a group of four. (The others are "Track," "Nostalgia," and "Black Spruce"; the last is a prose poem.) In each poem, the story revolves around an image: the family dog going out to meet the speaker's great-grandfather; an old clock, "the feathered ratchet" of the key turning in its gut. It is instructive to set "Robinson's Crossing" beside "Cashion Bridge," another poem that keeps returning to an image (the bridge). But while the earlier poem attempts to witness everything, hurtling through its long inventory of luminous garbage, setting all of it in the balance against failure, in the later poem, the metaphorical imagination is deliberately plain; the diction, demotic. "Robinson's Crossing" is an attempt to think about the problems of settler Canadians of European descent. Let us notice two moments in the poem: in a photograph of some settlers, "what draws the eye, almost / a double-take, are the tipis / in the distance, three of them, / white, smudged — a view the lens / could not pull into focus." On the other hand, there is the dirt behind the speaker's old house: "The smell / was mesmerizing: musty, sweet, / dank, clay-ey; green — / and with a shock I realized / what it was: the same smell / as my family." These two moments, held in tensed juxtaposition, display one of the problems: originally, Indigenous Canadians were at home here, and European settlers and their descendants have failed to pull this fact, the *meaning* of this fact, into focus; at its limit, this failure is the atrocity of colonialism. — And yet the families of these settlers have *made* a home here; the speaker's family has fed from this earth, has adopted its scent, "the body's scent ... / ... the one a dog / picks up."

ANIMISM. *Thirty-seven Small Songs & Thirteen Silences* is an animist's field guide. We cannot really appreciate these poems without the faith that all things are full of gods. The book's title alludes to Pablo Neruda's *Twenty Love Poems and a Song of Despair*, while Zwicky's small songs themselves feel closer to his elemental odes or Federico García Lorca's poems. "All the poems of deep song are magnificently pantheistic," writes García Lorca; "the poets ask advice from the wind, the earth, the sea, the moon, and things as simple as a violet, a rosemary, a bird." Zwicky has compared her small songs to "little pebbles, little shells … buttons in a button jar"; and has said that she means them to be read in "a casual handful."

If poetry had an essence, these small songs would be its distillate. Their defining features are attention to specificity, and metaphorical imagination. What is fascinating is how the exercises of attending and imagining, in these songs, pull in opposite directions (not unlike the two horns of the lyre). On the one hand, the small song recognizes that this thing, to which it is attending, is irreplaceably unique. ("Ontological attention," writes Zwicky, "is a response to particularity: *this* kingfisher, *this* lagoon, *this* slant-wise smoky West Coast rain.") On the other hand, when the small song bears witness to *this* thing, it points to its connexion with some *other* thing. ("Viewed in one light, *this*ness will appear to be a relational property.") The voice of the nuthatch is "beady and antique" — *like* the voice of a crumhorn.

Exhibit: "Small Song: Mozart." This small song is a good example of a poem that deserves close attention, and so may serve to remind us of the quality of attention equally due to Zwicky's other, longer poems.

Small Song: Mozart

Washing dishes after supper,
listening to the radio,
hands raised, mid-air,
the soap suds dripping …

What are you, music —
that in entering
undoes us? And undoing,
makes us whole.

Setting aside its images and themes — washing dishes, listening to Mozart, etc. — let us notice how this poem, like all good poems, lends itself to appreciation in terms of its prosody. This is a small song, not simply a small poem. Understanding its meaning is as much a matter of listening to *how* it says as it is of discerning *what*, exactly, it wishes to say. Notice the metrical patterns in the first stanza, each line composed as a variation of falling rhythms: a strong first stress followed by one or two soft stresses, so that the effect on the listener is like a quick intake of breath followed by exhalation. One rises, briefly, and then comes back down to earth. In the first line this pattern is manifest as a series of four trochees: a worker's rhythm — strong and laborious, and not unlike the domestic act of washing dishes. This pattern of stresses is varied in the second line: the strong first beat remains but the soft stresses are extended into a dactyl followed by a pyrrhic followed by another dactyl (LIstening to the RADio). Falling rhythms continue until the ellipsis at the close of the stanza.

The thematic shift to the second stanza is also a shift in music. The insistent falling rhythms give way to rising ones. There is an elegant symmetry, then, between the stanzas. If there is a connexion between the music of Mozart and the music of this poem, it is here in that symmetry. Moreover, also by analogy with Mozart's music, especially his string quartets, as the climax is approached, one feels lifted or raised; one does not return to the dishes or indeed to the domestic (a contrast with Haydn's music which Zwicky has noted elsewhere). It is possible still to hear trochees — scansion is not an objective science, in any case — but the dominant impression is that of rising iambs: what ARE you MUSic — / that in ENterING / unDOES us? And unDOing, / MAKES us WHOLE? The participles create an atmosphere of suspension: the speaker, who is implied but who never appears as a grammatical subject, is caught, paused, hands raised mid-air. The suspension is broken in the second stanza, just as the metrical pattern is broken, by the shift into the transitive verb. This shift also marks the moment of epiphany.

A variety of other prosodic devices work together to achieve this poem's musical coherence. The second stanza revolves around the long and short *u*, and the suffix *-ing*. The first stanza and the second are connected by the rhyming of "washing," "listening," "dripping" with "entering" and "undoing." There is also the understated assonance of "radio" and "makes us whole." These aural devices, along with the metrical variations, inform what is indeed a very tightly composed poem; its musical coherence suggests deep *semantic* coherence.

This brief analysis makes no attempt to paraphrase the content of the poem; and this silence is intentional. The commitment to clarity is at the centre of Zwicky's poetics. When we read her poetry, we might be cautious of the (understandable) urge to paraphrase. Instead, we might read her poetry as we might listen to the classical compositions with which her work keeps company. When we wish for further understanding or appreciation, we might try reading the poem again, slowly, and aloud — the literary equivalent of practising the fingering. Or we might brush up on our prosody. Or we might set the poem beside other, analogous poems. (A poem to set beside this one is "Small Song: Anger": the notes of the violin "dissolving / the knotted vines, the stems, / the hinges and the bars.")

EROS AND CONTEMPLATION. **Exhibits: "Music and Silence," "Envoy," and "The Art of Fugue."** In the most powerful poems in Zwicky's *Forge*, we hear the distilled intimacy and near-anonymity of lyric expression from her small songs (indeed, the collection includes a handful of small songs); but the scope of the form is expanded. The specificity of an imagistic constraint finds a place in longer poems and poetic suites. The philosophical and musical investigations conducted in *The New Room*, *Songs for the Relinquishing of the Earth*, and *Robinson's Crossing* continue here with fresh intensity; the voice of those earlier collections becomes almost orphic.

Notice the "restricted, echoic vocabulary" Zwicky employs in these poems, especially evident in the nouns: "wind," "light," "trees," "mountains," "water," and so on. Consider this stanza from the first variation of "Music and Silence":

> In the still light, you put your feet down,
> this one, that one, then this one,
> again on the yellow earth. Your happiness
> was like the trees': golden and tattered.

Or these lines from the first variation of "Envoy":

> ... your voice
> lifting in me like the wind, your touch
>
> breaking through me like rain,
> like sunlight. And the rain
>
> falling in the silence behind the broken wind.

Zwicky's repeated use of these nouns, her insistence upon them again and again, makes them assume the status of semantic chords; they are no more clichéd than, say, the chord of D minor. "The Art of Fugue" (its title borrowed from Bach's great unfinished composition) begins "A room, a table, and four chairs" — an initially unremarkable line using simple diction. The image is repeated in the second poem of the suite, and in the same position, but with a slight variation. The nouns are further recombined throughout the fugue. We are told, again in the first poem, "The chairs are made of wood, / the floor is wood, / the walls are bare." "West light" and "east light" are similarly repeated throughout, so that the fourth poem begins again with that simple diction: "West light, east light, a wooden table / and four chairs: multiple, multiple, multiple / are the voices of the inmost heart." But if we give attention to the fugue as a whole, we see that the diction is less simple than it is minimalist and restrained. The poems continue to think, to meditate on grief and selfhood, and these themes are formally realized in the music, and audible when we take seriously the notion that this fugue is governed by a composer's intuitions; and — more so than most poems — it approaches the condition of music.

Alternatively, the poems of this collection, so attentive to the wind and the light and the seasons, returning to the fundamentals of our experience with which those nouns are burdened, are comparable to Mark Rothko's mature paintings. His heavy primary colours, the repeating rectangles and squares, as if variations on a single vision, a continuous dusk or the sound of a foghorn. When we see his work on its own in a gallery, those paintings hung beside each other, we do not complain about their generality, as if the colour red, like the word "light," were unfit for meditative painterly treatment. Instead we are provoked, even dragged, into contemplation. What we witness there is very far from the minutiae of the merely private. We witness instead a testimony of the primary imagination.

> If what lay below was light.
> If what you could not find was there.
> If its hard fire was a golden river.
> If the golden river was a forge.
> If the forge was rock, and if the rock was shining.
> If the forge was love.

> — *Darren Bifford and Warren Heiti*
> *Saranda and Halifax*

Selected Bibliography

Benjamin, Walter. "On the Concept of History." *Selected Writings*. Vol. 4. Ed. Howard Eiland and Michael W. Jennings; trans. Edmund Jephcott et al. Cambridge: Belknap Press of Harvard University Press, 2003. 389–400.

Borson, Roo. *Personal History*. Toronto: Pedlar Press, 2008.

García Lorca, Federico. *In Search of Duende*. Ed. and trans. Christopher Maurer. New York: New Directions, 1998.

Glück, Louise. *Proofs & Theories*. Hopewell: Ecco Press, 1994.

Sinclair, Sue. "Red Pepper." *Secrets of Weather & Hope*. London, ON: Brick Books, 2001. 24.

Zwicky, Jan. "Bringhurst's Presocratics: Lyric and Ecology." *Poetry and Knowing*. Ed. Tim Lilburn. Kingston, ON: Quarry Press, 1995. 65–117.

ge. Kentville, NS: Gaspereau Press, 2011.

⸻. "The Geology of Norway: Poem with Introduction." *Harvard Review of Philosophy* VII (1999): 29–34.

⸻. "Imagination and the Good Life." *Common Knowledge* 20.1 (Winter 2014): 28–45.

⸻. *Lyric Philosophy*. 2nd edition. Kentville, NS: Gaspereau Press, 2011.

⸻. "Mathematical Analogy and Metaphorical Insight." *Mathematical Intelligencer* 28.2 (2006): 4–9.

⸻. *The New Room*. Toronto: Coach House Press, 1989.

⸻. Reading from *Thirty-seven Small Songs & Thirteen Silences*. Montreal: Atwater Poetry Project, 28 September 2007.

⸻. *Robinson's Crossing*. London, ON: Brick Books, 2004.

⸻. *Songs for Relinquishing the Earth*. London, ON: Brick Books, 1998.

⸻. *Thirty-seven Small Songs & Thirteen Silences*. Kentville, NS: Gaspereau Press, 2005.

⸻. *Wisdom & Metaphor*. 2nd edition. Kentville, NS: Gaspereau Press, 2008.

⸻. *Wittgenstein Elegies*. Coldstream: Brick Books / Edmonton: Academic Printing and Publishing, 1986.

Practising Bach

In the morning, sun fogged
in a crystal haze, two horses on the side road
the colour of old violins. Rhythm
is the spring in their step.
Over and over the steady repetition
till the fingers fall with a sureness
past control.

A plain man, uxorious.
The Brandenburg Concerti sent
but never opened. Unsung; the Art
of Fugue and sandwiches,
church organist, cantatas
on demand, and yet

these notes — their names
are stars. Our century is breath
on a winter night, or late thin
cloud, the moon. This music
is the earth's inaudible revolve
through space: horizon
draws back like a curtain.

The densest truths are home.
Liszt, Paganini, all the brilliant unreal
postures of intensity — nothing like
the dishes in the rack, heads raised
for the clear hot rinse, children
having their hair washed in the bath.

One cardinal, sweet against the snow
as candy, as a long-stemmed rose.
But it is sparrows who
are brown as bread, empty the feeder
hourly, divest us of those seeds:
smooth, striped,
unique and numberless as days.

Language Is Hands

Language visits the dentist: fevered
tooth to the world's
cold lunch. Twitchy, beaten yet again
by the unsayable, it's time
to scrape the nerve-pulp out, spirit
gone friable as ash.

In the desert of nth-order quantificational
logic and shopping malls, this is not
what Herakleitos meant. When you dry a plant out
water stays inside its soul like wisdom
in the muscles of a farmer's hand.
Language is a cactus.

Language is a hand, a hand
used to pulling on galoshes: ribbed nails, long thumb
that lies along a car door
like a donkey's ear against its neck.
Mottled skin and knobbiness unowned
anymore by anyone.

If it remembers hunger, it is
to touch, for tendons that flex and contract
into sound; to have been
a musician's hand with its cat-mind,
grasping the handle of a fridge door
the way a dancer walks in his body.

You poor old slipper, speech:
worn out, kicked off
for having failed, grown threadbare.
There may be no words for the vibratoless
baroque of the cello world, which you
have tried to show me, galloped

each day right up to the edge
of what Kant understood, wheeled in its face.
Yet I set you to the task again, against
yourself, and you struggle with the goodwill
of a later-to-be-schizophrenic child.
Like my dog, Sam,

who in an urgency of insight
drops his soggy tennis ball at my distracted feet,
and whom I banish, thankless, reading
not his terrible compassion but
mere need, bronzed to necessity; at best
irrelevant demand.

from Leaving Home

I

Once more, avocado, oldest friend,
into the breach: all seven leafless feet
crouched in the truck-box mid-way back
between the mat-wrapped table and the garbage pail,
a single bit of twine around your middle
knotted half-assed to a kitchen chair.
    Inverse of those chill nights
when we warded off the frost
with packing crates and blankets — excess
of domesticity, this cardboard-boxing
of a life.

I've moved too often now and with
too little consequence. But Charlie, you:
                    Minnesota,
                    Oregon by oxcart,
                    the Stanger sawmill,
                    the Mayerthorpe homestead.
Always in your pockets, seeds.

    First in the country to grow tomatoes —
all that patient fiddling with the glass-topped frame
against the south side of the pumphouse. Your fascination
with their sex.
                    And oaks. The strain you bred
survives up in the Peace.
The maples, lilacs, and the saskatoons; no one
loved squash so well as you and I.
Those trips, mid-winter, to the root house:
bins of plainer vegetables — carrots, parsnips,
big unwaxed Swedes, potatoes, red and white —
heaped in the dank. The flat lips

of fungi that protruded from the tunnel walls,
great bald albinos swung for a second
into the dim lantern beam.
'Close that door there, can't you?' muffled,
only four or five feet in; feeling it
come to with a snug thud
against my shoulder, ancient burlap
reeking.

But also, at the end,
wildflowers. It was after I had left
you rolled away the empty wheat and chop bins,
put the coop on skids and burnt it
in the draw. Took the fence down, useless
anyway: always there'd been chickens on the lawn
and in the lane up by the house.
It was quiet then, a little pocket in the scrub
emptied of cackle.
First you brought
tiger-lilies from the railroad ditch,
slowly stumping down the lane, orange heads
bobbing and flashing at each step, their roots
in plastic bags. Then cowslips, harebells, gentian,
wild columbine and dogwood. Haphazard,
they didn't always take; but mostly did
and needed little tending.
'Difference between a blessing and a curse
is knowing when to quit.'
After you died
it lasted several years, a swatch of coloured chaos
in the taffeta of leaves, until
the woods began to claim their own.
Hard to find now, occupants gone missing
one by one. Perhaps they've left for home.

II

Other things you almost taught me:
how to gentle down a frightened horse,
puncture the bristly stomach of a bloated calf,
grow barley in Northern Alberta gumbo —
that joke of a topsoil, slick cold soup
slopped over thousands of square miles of hardpan.
To love light the consistency of skim milk,
and muskeg scrub.
                            How to string barbed wire,
how to use a crosscut saw. To stand
with my hands in my back pockets. Amble.

    Half a continent between us on a May Day
    cold enough to do Alberta proud,
                            trilliums
    have bloomed in the woods behind this house.
    But though you gave me skill enough
    to grow the most cantankerous
    domestic plants, that white delicacy
    eluded both of us, time and again.
    You had to settle for a photograph,
    a thin black frameful on the kitchen wall.
    One of the few things packed
    into the cardboard box they gave us
    at the nursing home. The photographer
    has turned her back directly to the sun,
    they open to her, hundreds on hundreds
    of white ears, a mass of expectation
    cocked eternally against the glass.

Or
      to emerge at dusk from the woods,
sun cutting great fans of light across the lawn,
to hear music —
                  faint,
                  the same Schumann song
                  that one phrase
                              over and over, something dissolving
inside, a figure seen in half light through the screen door
leant forward, shadowed head
to the dark bloom of the gramophone,
                        im Blütenschimmer
                              durch die stillen Lande
the terrible astonishment of adulthood
all over your face.

            VIII

On every windowsill, pressed against the panes
or, now that it is spring occasionally a screen, plants:
frozen, mid-gesture, listening.
Streets vacant with lateness
and the rain — their element, no wonder
they are so intent.
                  In woods,
flowers have folded for the night. Brown boxes
yawn, cooling their heels in my kitchen.

What would it be, to have known love only
as a sheen of sound on pavement
or as that scent, odd, like moonlight
                              drifting
under something sealed
                  the shimmer of blossoms
                  the silent lands

from Seven Elegies: Robert William Zwicky (1927–1987)

The Horse Pull

The fairgrounds are deserted,
everywhere the sound of rain —
in the saplings near the show ring,
on the barn rooves. Of course
the team of Belgians
won. What could resist such
massive blondness? No, desire

is a Morgan horse,
bunched flanks slashed
by the sun; the taut suck
as a hoof slips; blood's
soundless nova, body
crashing to its knees; this fact,
this fact that will not move.

Your Body

Like that couple I heard about later
who hit a snowy owl one night in a storm
                    out of nowhere, huge, impossible
        velvet crunch jack-knifed back into the blizzard, good
        god, stopped somehow, dry-throated, half-knowing, scared
        to look, ashamed not to
                        — so,
it now seems to me, I arrived at the door of your room.

I can imagine them
not saying anything, sitting,
snow swirling in the headlights, wondering
how much blood, how broken, what if
it's still alive, what if it looks
at us. And then
instead, all that whiteness,
the immense plain of its fragility,
how the skin does actually hold the body in,
your arms like snapped lilacs, bruises
pooling at your elbows, ankles, knees,
the excellence of the skull,
its visible perfection, and everything
unclenching irretrievably in that moment so that

they, too, must have stooped,
                        the blue-edged carom of beauty
erupting through terror's grey prairie as a voice
floods, choking with praise:
                        lifts.

K. 219, Adagio

Now the sky above New Mexico
is hazy with Los Angeles, what words
will you invent for clarity?

Some things were always nameless:
the heart as rainbarrel,
the ear a long-stemmed glass.

The fiddle is still maple tuned with starlight,
the bow, breath with a backbone,
sweet with sap.

That long trill
is a hand that lifts your hair
a final time, sunlight, a last kiss

that knows it is the last.
And the phrase that follows:
a small voice talking to itself, how

some moments are so huge
you notice only little things:
nicks in the tabletop, the angle of a fork.

Drink. It
is what you will have
to remember:

rain's vowelless syntax,
how mathematics was an elegy,
the slenderness of trees.

The Geology of Norway

But when his last night in Norway came, on 10 December, he
greeted it with some relief, writing that it was perfectly possible that
he would never return.

— Ray Monk, *Ludwig Wittgenstein*

I have wanted there to be
no story. I have wanted
only facts. At any given point in time
there cannot be a story: time,
except as now, does not exist.
A given point in space
is the compression of desire. The difference
between this point and some place else
is a matter of degree.
This is what compression is: a geologic epoch
rendered to a slice of rock you hold between
your finger and your thumb.
That is a fact.
Stories are merely theories. Theories
are dreams.
A dream
is a carving knife
and the scar it opens in the world
is history.
The process of compression gives off thought.
I have wanted
the geology of light.

They tell me despair is a sin.
I believe them.
The hand moving is the hand thinking,
and despair says the body does not exist.
Something to do with bellies and fingers
pressing gut to ebony,

thumbs on keys. Even the hand
writing is the hand thinking. I wanted
speech like diamond because I knew
that music meant too much.

And the fact is, the earth is not a perfect sphere.
And the fact is, it is half-liquid.
And the fact is there are gravitational anomalies. The continents
congeal, and crack, and float like scum on cooling custard.
And the fact is,
the fact is,
and you might think the fact is
we will never get to the bottom of it,
but you would be wrong.
There is a solid inner core.
Fifteen hundred miles across, iron alloy,
the pressure on each square inch of its heart
is nearly thirty thousand tons.
That's what I wanted:
words made of that: language
that could bend light.

Evil is not darkness,
it is noise. It crowds out possibility,
which is to say
it crowds out silence.
History is full of it, it says
that no one listens.
The sound of wind in leaves,
that was what puzzled me, it took me years
to understand that it was music.
Into silence, a gesture.
A sentence: that it speaks.
This is the mystery: meaning.
Not that these folds of rock exist
but that their beauty, here,
now, nails us to the sky.

The afternoon blue light in the fjord.
Did I tell you
I can understand the villagers?
Being, I have come to think,
is music; or perhaps
it's silence. I cannot say.
Love, I'm pretty sure,
is light.
        You know, it isn't
what I came for, this bewilderment
by beauty. I came
to find a word, the perfect
syllable, to make it reach up,
grab meaning by the throat
and squeeze it till it spoke to me.
I wanted language
to hold me still, to be a rock,
I wanted to become a rock myself. I thought
if I could find, and say,
the perfect word, I'd nail
mind to the world, and find
release.
The hand moving is the hand thinking:
what I didn't know: even the continents
have no place but earth.

These mountains: once higher
than the Himalayas. Formed in the pucker
of a supercontinental kiss, when Europe
floated south of the equator
and you could hike from Norway
down through Greenland to the peaks
of Appalachia. Before Iceland existed.
Before the Mediterranean
evaporated. Before it filled again.
Before the Rockies were dreamt of.
And before these mountains,

the rock raised in them
chewed by ice that snowed from water
in which no fish had swum. And before that ice,
the almost speechless stretch of the Precambrian:
two billion years, the planet
swathed in air that had no oxygen, the Baltic Shield
older, they think, than life.

So I was wrong.
This doesn't mean
that meaning is a bluff.
History, that's what
confuses us. Time
is not linear, but it's real.
The rock beneath us drifts,
and will, until the slow cacophony of magma
cools and locks the continents in place.
Then weather, light,
and gravity
will be the only things that move.

And will they understand?
Will they have a name for us? — Those
perfect changeless plains,
those deserts,
the beach that was this mountain,
and the tide that rolls for miles across
its vacant slope.

ms' Clarinet Quintet in B Minor, Op. 115

That we shall not forget to honour
brown, its reedy clarities.

And, though the earth is dying
and the names of its diseases
spread from the fencelines, Latinate:
a bright field
ribboned with swath.

That the mind's light could be filtered
as: a porch, late afternoon,
a trellised rose,
                    which is to say
a truth in nostalgia:
if we steel ourselves against regret
we will not grow more graceful,
but less.

That a letter might honestly
begin, *Dear beloved.*

Cashion Bridge

It would be as well at the outset to admit
how even to have said this much
is to have failed. That the moment that I want to slow into slow-
    motion,
hold up to the light, not in stop-time but in the starry leak of
    epochs, the light
that floats in the apse of Salisbury, that ebbs north from Churchill in
    October,
the light that dark remembers,
has already passed. In that light, this moment:
hands poised above the keys, bow at the apex of its arc toward the
    string
— last night someone was coughing, my neighbour
shifted in his seat — but it was that moment
that we'd come for, the one
most full of silence, fingers stretching through it to —
                                      well,
what? the piece? the *thing*?
                            — but by then, the light's
snapped on, the note has flashed and risen
like the downstroke of the nib, dawn slicing the horizon,
the paddle breaking through the surface, scarring it
with light. Hegel wrote:
not curiosity, not vanity,
not the consideration of expedience, not duty or conscience
but an unquenchable unhappy thirst that brooks no compromise
leads us to truth. He also wrote:
only by understanding what it's not
can we come to understand what something is.
This is the difficulty of beginnings.

    You are walking west.
    The elderberry's turned, and some branches of the maples at
        Kennedy's

are bronze: the colour's dull this year because of drought.
The Glover's new canes have come on, though —
just enough rain at the right time; earlier
they lost the old canes and the crop.
Old Mr. Irvine's lane, Dave Petepiece's,
then his brothers' driveways: their mother died
last month: looks like, out back,
someone is learning how to drive.
The stretch down the far side of the rise, scotch pine
and two oaks on the north, a maple on the south,
people we don't know in the place set back from the road.
Up the next rise, Spillers, new,
from Montreal, and the people with the big dog
on the right. The blank unwindowed barn —
and odourless — along the left. Then
cornfields; more cornfields; and the shingle-sided shack,
we don't know who, red window-frames and plastic on the
          windows,
and you're at the Cashion sideroad.
                            South
takes you to the swamp — the unofficial
dump — and then across abandoned tracks
down to the Glen: narrow, bush-lined, not kept up, much used
by traffickers in U.S. contraband.
North, the sideroad's wider,
white with gravel, though I've never met a car.
An open field of corn on the east side, and on the west
a meadow, heavy with alsike and alfalfa,
and a hardwood bush that rises on the fencelines to the west
          and north;
in fact, the last few hundred feet you walk through shade
after mid-day, though I don't know how far west
the patch of trees extends: as far as you can see, from the bridge,
but the river bends just upstream
and it's hard to tell.

But this isn't
what I meant to try to say:
it's the starting out
I do not understand.
Years earlier, after midnight in a different province,
the gravel drops away in front of us. You can smell
the water: *Lights Off*
While Waiting For The Ferry: but no red-green
wink to say they've seen us from the other side: windows down,
a transport passing on the highway back of us, reeds
shifting slightly in the breeze,
then still again.
We flick our lights.
No shout, no quiver in the tow line,
just the little ridge of stones and sand shoved up
where the ramp has butted on the shore.
It's hard to give up — the town we live in visible, just there,
but forty minutes by the nearest bridge;
exhaustion hours old.
One sees with the greatest clarity,
sees nothing.

          I don't know
how many times I've walked to Cashion Bridge.
There are other lovely walks, of course,
and often I will wander east, or south,
or off along the tracks to town.
But this is my favourite. It's odd I've never
set foot on the other side; though I've noticed
you can hear, or even in the distance see,
the flit of cars or half-tons on the South Branch.
I miss the old boards: this version of the bridge
is new, they built it now a few years back.
The concrete gleams, white like the gravel,
where it's not in shade. I sit

the drain, against the balustrade along the west.
      :og or turtle drops into the water
under me, among the reeds. A clump of perfect cat-tails,
three straight and two a little bowed. The willows stretching out
        across the water,
currentless and brown.
                              But this isn't
what I meant to tell you either. What I wanted
was the walking, not the walking-to but
the not-getting-there, the every moment
starting out, the every moment
being lifted in an arc against the moment of arrival: the anticipation
is terrific, yet always nothing
happens when I'm there — so
not even this, but the ungraspableness
of knowing, the inarticulateness of
that flexed second above the keys,
of how we are translated,
                              that held breath
between the future and the past that's neither, but is still
the only place we'll ever be arriving
to, the only place it's possible
we are.

        Five o'clock on a rainy day.
Waking, with suddenness, to the open window.
Almost, you remember what it was like
when the future was ahead of you,
when the distant sound of the highway through the wet leaves
was the sound of a world
being invented.
              Yesterday,
on the radio, Bruckner's Second, clearing up the stuff from lunch
and there it was: the image of existence
being wrung out like a dishcloth in those chords, that
torqued crazy counterpoint, the name
of something language wants but cannot find the words

to say, that mash of semitones
the echo of the pressure from the other side,
the everything that what is isn't, its brink
the outline of the moment
of the hands above the keys — I think of Bruckner
walking that knife-edge
singing, and I am inclined
            to meet my class in rags, I am inclined
            to break down in the street,
            to wish for hurricanes,
            I am inclined to write my friends on placemats from the
                  Chinese take-out,
            to tell someone, anyone, what I really think.
So we might begin.

                  That room you've
            lived in summers, from which you've started out:
            the chair sits, turned a little sideways from the desk,
            in silence now. The window
            closed. Light falls through the curtains:
            it is dust. Each day
            the air grows imperceptibly more still
            and cold.
                  What is this, that looks
            so much like loyalty? Thinking that the future, your return,
            will give this present meaning
            is just one more gesture of possession: imagining
            the emptiness as loss, as failure, a stutter
            in the pure trajectory of occupation — no, what I mean is
            yes, it is a failure, of course it's failure,
            but not the one we think it is.
                              For that is what
            the world has been: not
            what we thought.
            Kant, Hegel, Heidegger,
            the ghosts of Descartes — thinking
            we are being's origin

is trying to become
its end. Bruckner was right: the world
is always letting go, it is
the moment of the hands above the keys,
the silence of beginning.
On the bridge, sun stammering through the willow leaves,
     white,
yellow, gold, is the futureless unnarrative of light, the every
     moment
starting out, staring straight up into it, being stared into,
fiery, hammering, light like trumpets, the cells
of your body alight, your mouth
open and disintegrating.
                 That last afternoon
we drove in the opposite direction — east first, then crossed
the Raisin at the Glenbrook bridge,
hauling thirty years, five families, from the attic and the cellar
to the township dump. Abandoning it there
at the lip of that huge scree
the way we know the world
will soon abandon us. But the world
knows otherwise: knows
even history is merely mortal,
and that the shrugging-off of ownership is other than
the letting-go of love, which is every moment turning from
the green translucent garden hose, the box of bathroom tiles,
the beauty of the comic books and drawers of kitchen clutter: corks,
     sealer lids, can-openers, bent straws and butter knives;
the lawnchair webbing, and the lawnchair frames, torn mattresses
     and bedsteads, the beauty of the plastic kitchen chairs;
a lampshade with pressed forget-me-nots and pansies,
wicker plantstands, birdfeeders, the Encyclopaedia Brittanica *Dama to
     Educ* and *Text to Vasc*, the complete symphonies of Beethoven,
a rubber boot, stoves, fridges, eavestroughing, roll-up blinds, end
     tables, tires, their beauty, shingles,
stuff in jars; and the beauty of dead trees, loose cushions and a box

of 1922 Ontario Readers, the beauty
of jumbles of clothesline, broken cinder block, barbed wire coils and
    television aerials,
of two pots without their lids, a pink blanket, gas cans, stuffed toys
    and bedsprings;
of the sea of garbage bags, the bobbing green, black, blue, and orange
    garbage bags;
and boxes of shirts and sweaters, trousers, rags, unrecyclable plastic:
    sheets
crumpled in the mass of things; bleach bottles, rolls of wall-to-wall;
the beauty of the chesterfields with matching chairs, the leather
    Lazyboy with stuffing coming out its arm,
the sheen on the stacks of rotting newsprint, phonebooks, velvet paint-
    by-number sets; the broken patio umbrella, children's bicycles;
and the bits of dowelling, radiant, the broken quarter round and
    two-by-fours with peeling paint, the gleam
of momentariness, throat raised, the knife edge
incandescent with its failure, knowing itself failed,
and singing.

Bill Evans: "Here's That Rainy Day"

On a bad day, you come in from the weather
and lean your back against the door.
This time of year it's dark by five.
Your armchair, empty in its pool of light.

That arpeggio lifts, like warmth, from the fifth of B minor,
offers its hand — *let me*
tell you a story ... But in the same breath,
semitones falling to the tonic:
you must believe and not believe;
that door you came in
you must go out again.

In the forest, the woodcutter's son
sets the stone down from his sack and speaks to it.
And from nothing, a spring wells,
falling as it rises, spilling out
across the dark green moss.
There is sadness in the world, it says,
past telling. Learn stillness
if you would run clear.

Beethoven: Op. 95

> *Nel mezzo del cammin di nostra vita*
> *mi retrovai per una selva oscura*

I

An apology, first: I did not guess
the moodiness my middle years
would bring, unschooled as I was
in the varieties of frustration.
You were right: stupidity
surrounds us, and our own
splits the skull most sharply.
Also: that nothing
is achieved without the grimmest labour
on the slenderest of hopes
(except perhaps for Wolfgang, who was not
entirely human).
Not even music comes in its own words.

The importance of walks,
your duty to your nephew,
and the muscle in a true *cantabile*: you were right
about discipline, and politics,
the steep well of fury, and finally
what the fury goes through to: love
like a hand through the wall of the chest,
like a hand in fire, fire
tearing itself, in the hand's flame
a heart, in the heart's fist
an ear.

II

Remember this one?
Twenty-six miles he runs, in the sun,
Marathon to Athens, his heart
punching the blood through his lungs, runs
it will turn out — though he
won't live to know this — to announce
the dawning of the Golden Age.

The walls, and then the gate;
and the news that he has come
spreading before him like
the bright pool from a sacrifice, and still
he runs: to the agora,
to the Council Chamber, now
someone has recognized him and it's guessed
what news he brings; he slows — the crowd
behind him, shifting, tense — hauls
hugely on the air, roars *joy*,
we are victorious
and drops dead.

It's beside the point
the story is apocryphal. Myth is history
we need. And what matters is
the bit off camera,
not a goatherd or a guide car in sight,
around mile twenty, say, when the message
could be anything: the truth
has struck his body — *this*
cannot be done — but he takes
the next step anyway. Not out of loyalty
or pride, but because he is a runner,
and he wills it. And what matters is

some facts exhaust us this way, too.
We fight until the spirit's stripped,
nothing between us and the bare floor of the self, and then
the thing that cannot happen
happens, the thing that no one sees:
some place past emptiness
we take another step.

III

Hearing, you have reached the end,
the kernel bitter in your mouth.
Where would you go
even if your throat would open?
Only in the country,
relief (o, in the country!) — as if
every tree spoke.

If all comes to naught,
if all comes to naught ...
All is coming to naught,
but the earth, sweet stillness,
remains, will remain. Woods,
hearing stillness, remain ...

This plague, my hearing.
Only in the country, praise.
Only on the earth, sweetness.
Music, this sweetness,
deer in the twilight:
o hearing, o earth,
remain.

IV

A walk in autumn fields, the smell
of hay and dust not unlike
a canvas tent. In a year of downpours,
a week without rain: grasshoppers
bounce off through the weeds like coins.
A breeze in the blaze of aspens;
sun hums in the frozen sweep of spruce.

You are tired,
like the dry earth.
But unlike it
you know too much.
For still, that is
earth's definition:
whatever it knows,
that is enough.

And because it is fall,
darkness will shadow the northwest;
and because it is late in this century,
darkness will be in the air you breathe.
And because you are human, darkness
has come from your hand,
your mouth,
and it thickens around your heart
like fat around a liver: you will never
know enough.

            For you are alive:
here, sitting in the dirt,
the clumps of shorn alfalfa,
the crack in the dust,
hay down your collar, a wasp, the aspens
luminous, the luminous sky
big as an outflung arm.

For this is the world:
even you, with your hands, and your language,
and your fat black heart.

And the light,
the light shines on it.

      v

And I misread the coda, too:
thought you thought
you'd heard some angel
clattering on the stairs.

But no.
The floundering, the rage, fistfuls
of wrong-shaped emptiness: you knew
as well as anyone.
God comes from the darkness —
if he comes —
like pain from a wound,
frost from concrete,
the next step.

Which is not to say
there is no joy — only that
it's never a reward.
That's all you meant:
the sweetest truth, or the most terrible,
can fly up, just like that, be lost
like dust in sunlight.

Driving Northwest

Driving northwest in July before
the long twilight that stretches into
the short summer dark, despite the sun
the temperature is dropping, air
slips by the truck, like diving,
diving,
          and you are almost blind
with light: on either side of you
it floats across the fields, young barley
picking up the gold, oats white,
the cloudy bruise of alfalfa
along the fencelines, the air itself
tawny with haydust, and the shadows of the willows
in the draw miles long, oh it is lovely
as a myth, the touch of a hand on your hair,
and you need, like sleep, to lie down now
and rest, but you are almost
blind with light, the highway
stretched across the continent
straight at the sun: visor,
dark glasses, useless against its gonging,
the cab drowns in it, shuddering, you cannot tell,
you might be bleeding or suffocating, shapes
fly out of it so fast there's no time to swerve:
but there is no other path, there is no other bed,
it is the only way home you know.

Prairie

And then I walked out into that hayfield west of Brandon,
evening, late July, a long day in the car from Nipissing
and long days in the car before that; the sun
was red, the field a glow of pink, and the smell of the grasses
and alfalfa and the sleek dark scent of water nearby ...
I remember — now — chasing something underneath the farmhouse
      table as a child
and seeing the big hasp on the underside that locked the two main
      leaves: it seemed
rough and enormous, out of keeping with the polished surfaces
it held together, almost medieval, I was startled and a bit afraid; and later
as an adult, fumbling for it, blind, at the limits of my reach,
how finally it would let go with a sharp jerk and the leaves
would sigh apart: but it was there,
in that hayfield, that I felt some rusty weight in my chest stick
then give, a slow opening to sky —
                            it was that hasp, I know it now,
though at the time I did not recognize I was remembering,
nor, had you told me, would I then have known why.

Epistemology

If you do know that here is one hand, *we'll grant you all the rest.*
—Ludwig Wittgenstein

Because there were no hands, they were
completely absent. I don't mean this as a joke. Nothing
prepared me for it: it was like a dream.
That's why. Because I've tried hard to forget.
And, without warning, I could tell that I was
seven storeys in the air. The fragrance of the earth
when I lay down on it. Because
I'd pulled the fuses from my heart
and every corridor was suddenly ablaze.
Because things like that don't happen on the bus.
I mean that when I stepped out on that plain,
I'd been alone for years — it was
the breath of spring, and it was snowing.
Because it was a river in my heart, because
it moved like winter underneath my skin. A tree
came into leaf behind my eyes.
It woke me up.
The silence sparkled. Imagine
singing without sound, because it was
like that; and when I think of it at lunch,
Liz, Shelley talking about movies, Gerry
hockey, Bruce about the mayonnaise,
I start to cry. Because my body
was a flock of horned larks and my bones were
bells. It didn't care — that's how I knew.
Because it was the opening of an eye. And, yes:
because it was against all reason.

One Version

after Paul Hindemith, Funf Stücke, *No.4*

Someone walks alone
under the sky. The sky
is grey, like history. The walker
wears an overcoat but it's
no use: the cold
turns to metal in his joints, noiselessly,
the way it slicks the sky.
Nothing moves: the walker,
who is walking, does not move. That's
history for you. Did I mention
that the walker's back
is to us, collar turned up, that he
wears a hat? Still,
we know everything. We have forgotten
when it was we last slept.
Did I mention we have lost
our eyelids. Did I mention
that the distance lengthens
every step, that every step the distance
stays the same.

Robinson's Crossing

They say
the dog was crazy that whole evening:
whining at the door, tearing
around the yard in circles,
standing stock still in the cart track,
head cocked, whimpering.
They'd left him out and gone to bed, but he
kept barking until after midnight
when they finally heard him take off
down the railbed, east,
toward the river. Next morning
Ernest said he'd met him
a half-mile from the house. The train
had got in late but he'd
been eager to get home, so walked
the eight miles from the crossing
at the steel's end. They had finished
with the harvest down south, he had money
in his pocket. He was
two days early,
but the dog had known.

My great-
grandmother slept
in a boxcar on the night
before she made the crossing. The steel
ended in Sangudo then, there was
no trestle on the Pembina, no siding
on the other side. They crossed
by ferry, and went on by cart through bush,
the same eight miles. Another
family legend has it that she stood there

in the open doorway of the shack
and said, "You told me, Ernest,
it had windows and a floor."

           The museum
has a picture of the Crocketts —
later first family of Mayerthorpe —
loading at the Narrows
on the trail through Lac Ste. Anne.
Much what you'd expect:
a wagon, crudely covered,
woman in a bonnet on the box seat,
man in shirt sleeves
by the horses' heads, a dog.
But what draws the eye, almost
a double-take, are the tipis
in the distance, three of them,
white, smudged — a view the lens
could not pull into focus.
And another photo,
taken in the '30s maybe,
of a summer camp down on the river flats
between our quarter and the town.
At least a dozen tipis; horses, smoke.
By the time I was a kid,
they'd put the town dump there;
but I remember we picked arrowheads
out of the west field every spring
when it was turned. And a memory
of my uncle, sharp, impatient with
my grandfather for lending out
his .22 to Indians:
last time, didn't he remember?,
he never got it back.

Robinson's Crossing
is how you come in to this country, still —
though it's not been on a map
since 1920, and the highway
takes a different route. You come in,
on the backs of slightly crazy Europeans, every time
you lift your eyes across a field of swath
and feel your throat catch
on the west horizon. It's the northern edge
of aspen parkland here —
another ten miles down the track,
the muskeg's getting serious.
But my great-grandfather was right:
cleared, seeded, fenced,
trees left for windbreaks and along
the river's edge, it looks
a lot like England.
You could file
on a quarter section for ten dollars;
all you had to do to keep it
was break thirty acres in three years.
The homestead map shows
maybe two in three men
made it. Several of their wives
jumped from the bridge.

There's no mention
in the local history book
of how the crossing got its name.
I found a picture of an Ernie
Robinson — part of a road gang
in the '20s — and of an old guy,
Ed, at some town function
later on. There's also
a photo of a sign, undated, shot
from an extreme low angle, as though

whoever took it had been standing
in the ditch beside the grade. I'll show you
where it was: just go out
the old road from the RV park, west,
about two miles. Nothing there now
but a farmer's crossing and a stretch
of old rail in the ditch. I'm guessing
that they closed it
when the steel moved on
after the war.

           A few years back
I was out behind the old house
picking twigs. (TransAlta
had come in and taken out
a poplar — it had left
enough junk in the grass
my mother couldn't mow.)
The rake had clawed
the grass out, more than
it had piled up twigs,
so I was squatting, sorting
dirt and grass by hand. The smell
was mesmerizing: musty, sweet
dank, clay-ey; green —
and with a shock I realized
what it was: the same smell
as my family. Not because
our boots and gloves
were covered in it, nothing
you could shower off — it was
the body's scent, the one
that's on the inside
of your clothes, the one a dog
picks up. Our cells were
made of it: the garden, and the root

cellar, the oats
that fed the chickens, and the hay
the steers.
   These days

the line north of the farmhouse
carries only freight,
infrequently; the highway's
being twinned; Monsanto
just released another herbicide-resistant
seed. Before the drought,
the river flooded every time it rained —
no trees upstream; this year
it's lower than it's been
since someone started
keeping records. The wooden
elevators, gone or going; ranks
of concrete silos that read
Agricore in flowing nineteenth-century
script — it's why

the story matters, why it
puzzles me. Here comes
my great-grandfather, he has made
Robinson's Crossing, he is walking
toward us, bone-tired
but whistling, it's a fine night, he has
money in his pocket,
and the dog, the family dog,
is going out to meet him.

History

after J.S. Bach, Concerto in D Minor, BWV 1052

Someone is running
fingers through their hair.
The fingers
are like fish, they flicker
upstream while the current
purls around their backs
and falls away.
The fish

resemble wind inside a field
of wheat, resemble
solar flares, the fish
are water
that is trying to flow
up itself, the gravity
that hauls and tumbles it

deaf as the grief
inside perfection.
Do not ask.
You are running fingers
through your hair. This
is what you do sometimes
because you cannot put your hands
around your heart.

Another Version

Look, all I can tell you is
there was a car, big, dark blue,
a late-'40s Ford sedan; and rain,
and getting stuck, and rain and rain.
Forcing the back door wide enough
to struggle out, the ruts
shin-high, the gumbo
slick and shiny in the half-light,
gunmetal, the wet-iron
smell of it.
And how it packed itself
like pie dough in the wheelwells,
the scuffed burr of the spinning tires,
the men cursing and grunting as they rocked it,
exhaust thickening the drizzle
and the hubcap logo stopping upside
down, then right side up, then
upside down. And that we had to wait
until the tractor
came: the clank-whump
as the chain drew taut, the lunge,
the heave, the drunken
fishtail as we broke
the suck; and maybe also, thinking
even then that we'd misunderstood,
had failed to grasp the meaning
of that monstrous union between
car and road, its refusal
of intent.
As though they knew, wanted
to save us. And we drove on.

Glenn Gould: Bach's "Italian" Concerto, BWV 971

[handwritten annotation: amphibrac]

North of Superior, November,
bad weather behind, more
coming in from the west, the car windows furred
with salt, the genius of his fingers
bright, incongruous, cresting a ridge
and without warning the sky
has been swept clear: the shaved face
of the granite, the unleafed aspens
gleaming in the low heraldic light, the friend
I had once who hoped he might die
listening to this music, the way
love finds us in our bodies
even when we're lost. I've known very little,
but what I have known
feels like this: compassion without mercy,
the distances still distances
but effortless, as though for just a moment
I'd stepped into my real life, the one
that's always here, right here,
but outside history: joy
precise and nameless as that river
scattering itself among
the frost and rocks.

[handwritten annotations in right margin: dactyl / (falling foot); (Associated w/ Elegiac, epic poetry); (Speak'n); My mistress' eyes are nothing / like the / sun]

Small song in praise of ears

Ah, my mushrooms,
my little fishes!
They laugh
when I tell them
you are beautiful.
Ah, my pink mice,
my infant trolls!

But who among them
has drunk dawn with its
thrush-scented air?
Who but you
has fingered silence,
that dark jewel
burning at night's throat.

Small song for the voice of the nuthatch

Such a brilliant day,
the sycamores
bronze rapids overhead,

and that tiny crumhorn
up there somewhere,
beady and antique.

The autumn light has such long legs
you'd fall in love, but it keeps
gazing off into the distance.

What distance?

Listen to the nuthatch: go home,
make bread, make soup.
Leave one chink open to the wind.

Small Song: Prairie

Wood light, meadow light,
the fencepost silver
in the afternoon's long stare;
beast light, the satin flash
of horserump or the brown hand
in the saskatoons;
cloud light and willow light,
the dead light of the salt marsh
and the hammered brilliance
of the dugout under wind;
even the rain in its night singing,
the night rain in its forgetting,
is a kind of light.

Small song to oneself

The tall sea comes
in the clothes of night,
it comes in the afternoon, brilliant
in the rags of grief.
It raises lace-gloved hands
among the rocks and weeds, and beckons
at your feet.

Do not go, do not go,
you who have loved the trees
which love the air.
You who have had to wait
for dawn before,
that bare light
not yet sweet with birds.

all Song: Mozart

Washing dishes after supper,
listening to the radio,
hands raised, mid-air,   ← spondee
the soap suds dripping …

What are you, music —
that in entering
undoes us? And undoing,
makes us whole.

Small Song: Laundry

Bellied out, aloft, and flush with sun,
like meadow-mist beside the morning river:
how tired we made you!
And how tired we had become.

Now, emptied of our restlessness,
you breathe your own white life.
— And there, like ghosts of meadow-grass,
our shadows shining through.

from Music and Silence: Seven Variations

I

Who can name the absence
music is, who draw that space,
the cold breath, sudden and empty
that will own you the rest of your life?

In the still light, you put your feet down,
this one, that one, then this one,
again on the yellow earth. Your happiness
was like the trees': golden and tattered.

Who could you have told? Leaves
fell around you, half shrug, half sorrow.
And the wind sprang up off the water
riding you, fierce, unbiddable, already lost.

IV

The pool stretched from the shallow steps behind the house.
You hadn't noticed until after you arrived
that it was dusk. And how the land on all sides
dropped away: miles to the valley floor.

The figure stepped out from your body,
arced above the surface, dove.
You might have stood forever, silence
shawling through the air like snow.

Crystal: blue: lit somewhere
from inside its depths. Even then
you didn't want to understand.
Even then, you knew.

V

All day, the winter light comes striding
down the strait and through the window.
Golden, thick with silence, and you
not knowing how to walk or speak.

This is your perplexity:
was it a hand
that reached up, plucked the arrow
in mid-flight? Or were you all along

arriving here, sidelong, failed,
but currented? A reason
would release you: this is how you know
it won't be found.

VII

That sound: something in you has been ringing ever since.
And you, stumbling at the edges of your self,
deaf, bewildered. Was it joy?
You were smaller than dust, dumb

as pebbles. Yes, you'd hoped your throat
would fill, your lungs. But you were
emptier than winter, defenceless.
You could not even tell yourself. And it was then

the flame inside you stood straight up,
tall, gold-coloured; and your heart walked forward
easily, as though something had called it, laid itself
on the anvil of that silence.

Late Schubert

A warm night in autumn, summery,
lying on the bed upstairs, a dog
barking somewhere in the distance: you are thinking
of your childhood, your long-dead father, or not
thinking so much as letting them
nudge up against you, boats
moored at the same dock on a still night, and a wavelet
made by who knows what wake, what storm, lifts them gently,
       briefly,
together, air glassy with calm, the moon
staring down. Isn't love
always like this? — A spider's thread, spindrift
with the tensile strength of steel. The light must fall
just so to make it visible, faint gleam
twisting above you, pulling
from so deep, so far back, you think it must be anchored
some place before you were born.
                        And the fever,
the restlessness, the way the heart surges
against the breakwater, plunges,
and surges again: isn't this
the same thing? — Love
afraid it won't get home, afraid
it will forget. Is dying
that hard? Its horizon
is the same shape as your life — wild hillsides
pointing to the wind, the sea
heaving under the sky's emptiness.
                      Let your hand
move into that darkness above your face: almost
you can feel the stars —
                their silence,
steady on the other side.

Practising Bach

*for performance with Bach's E Major
Partita for Solo Violin,* BWV 1006

PRELUDE

There is, said Pythagoras, a sound
the planet makes: a kind of music
just outside our hearing, the proportion
and the resonance of things — not
the clang of theory or the wuthering
of human speech, not even
the bright song of sex or hunger, but
the unrung ringing that
supports them all.

The wife, no warning, dead
when you come home. Ducats
in the fishheads that you salvage
from the rubbish heap. Is the cosmos
laughing at us? No. It's saying

improvise. Everywhere you look
there's beauty, and it's rimed
with death. If you find injustice
you'll find humans, and this means
that if you listen, you'll find love.
The substance of the world is light,
is water: here, clear
even when it's dying; even when the dying
seems unbearable, it runs.

LOURE

Why is Bach's music more like speech than any other? Because of its wisdom, I think. Which means its tempering of lyric passion by domesticity, its grounding of the flash of lyric insight in domestic earth, the turf of dailiness.

Let us think of music as a geometry of the emotions. Bach's practice, then, resembles that of the Egyptians: earth's measure as a way of charting the bottomlands of the Nile, the floodwaters of the heart, as a way of charting life. Opera, Greek tragedy, Romantic poetry tell us that sex and death are what we have to focus on if we want to understand any of the rest. Bach's music, by contrast, speaks directly to, and of, life itself — the resonant ground of sex and death.

And it does this not without ornamentation, but without fuss: the golden ratio in the whelk shell lying on the beach, the leaf whorl opening to sun, the presence of the divine in the chipped dish drying in the rack, *that* miracle: good days, bad days, a sick kid, a shaft of sunlight on the organ bench. *Talk to me, I'm listening.*

GAVOTTE

E major: June wind
in the buttercups, wild
and bright and tough.
Like luck — a truth
that's on the surface of a thing,
not because it's shallow, but because
it's open: overtoned.
Because it rings.
          Fate, too,
is character. But it's
the shape — the cadence
and the counterpoint. Luck
lives in the moment, and it
looks at you: the clear eye,
gold, when being sings.

MENUET I & II

There's nothing special in it. All you have to do
is hit the right key at the right time. Time:
that stream in which we do, and do not,
live. *Just practise diligently; it will all go well. You have*
five fingers on each hand, each one as healthy as my own.
Unison, the octave; the fifth, the fourth, the third.
Of the strings? The viola, if I have a choice.
At the keyboard, don't forget to use your thumb.
God's glory and the recreation of the mind.
What I really need to know:
does the organ have good lungs?
The partita of the world, the dance of being: *everything*
has to be possible.

BOURÉE

Partita, partie — a whole of many parts. Pythagoras, who is said to
have studied with the Egyptians, is also said to have taught that
enlightenment meant solving the problem of the One and the Many,
of coming to grasp the divine unity of the world through its bits and
pieces, as these come to us in language.

This may also be thought of as the problem of metaphor:
that metaphor's truth, its charge of meaning, depends on the
assertion of identity and difference, on erotic coherence and
referential strife, on meaning as resonance and meaning revealed
through analysis.

Lyric poets are always trying to approach the issue by
forcing speech to aspire to the condition of music. Bach comes at it
from the other end: he infuses music with a sense of the terrible
concreteness, the particularity, of the world. And enlightenment? —
Acceptance of, delight in, the mystery of incarnation.

GIGUE

There is a sound
that is a whole of many parts,
a sorrowless transparency, like luck,
that opens in the centre of a thing.
An eye, a river, fishheads, death,
gold in your pocket, and a half-wit
son: the substance of the world
is light and blindness and the measure
of our wisdom is our love.
Our diligence: ten fingers and
a healthy set of lungs. Practise
ceaselessly: there is
one art: wind
in the open spaces
grieving, laughing
with us, saying
improvise.

Gemini

after J.S. Bach, Cello Suite No. 5 in
C Minor, BWV 1011, Sarabande

There is a life
in which I do not find you.

Handedness that does not know
it's paired, a voice
that does not recognize
its line as counterpoint.

As though I were to learn
the air through which I'd grown
had not been fluid, making room
for me, but that my life
had curled and trellised on
some absent shape of emptiness
that had the shape of you.

The stories of Stickwalking
God, or One-Side: half a man,
one leg, one arm. And yet
he is a marksman
and a hunter. Spear points. Tips.

His half a heart and
its unbroken love. They say
it leaps out from his side
each time it beats.

If There Were Two Rivers

If there were two rivers.
If their water were clear gold.
If it were a flood, a homecoming, and where they joined,
        a standing wave, its crest of white.
If you climbed the hill alone, returning,
        and the grass was golden in the evening light.
If the golden water leaked around your feet
        out of the earth.
If it was everywhere you stepped — gold, streaming,
        and the clear light going down.
If, in the other dream, the children ran away.

If it were a ship, and the evening light at sea.
If it were a church, and the orange light of evening.
If there were no roof or walls.
If it was made of fire.
If it were radiant.
If it were massive, weightless, and a white fire
        misting from its centre like a breath.
If the rock was raw but glistening.
If it lit the foyer — if the light were all below and
        the other rooms were dusk.
If what happened was: you stood there.
If there was nothing to be said.

If it glowed.
If the glow was like a silent speech.
If the light was like a haze, a mist: if every detail
        were exact.
If it broke you open.
If your blood shone on the hearth.
If the silence deafened you.
If what you saw was the necessity.
If the hammer of it brought you to your knees.
If the hammer of it clove your heart.

If what lay below was light.
If what you could not find was there.
If its hard fire was a golden river.
If the golden river was a forge.
If the forge was rock, and if the rock was shining.
If the forge was love.

From Distant Lands

after Robert Schumann, Kinderszenen, *Op. 15*

Or was it a gust of wind? I had been walking
as I always walked, along that hallway, a place
I'd passed each day for years and never noticed,
thinking about summer, thinking
about sunlight, the anonymity of love: and then
you touched me — did you touch me? —
and the door I'd never seen swung back, flew open
and the wind that swept its hand across my face
passed by.
        And on the other side — the plain wood
of that casing, the simple latch — not
an attic, not a cloakroom, but
a castle: oak and glass and polished stone.
It was caverned, glistening, windows
with the loft of mountain air and floors
like northern lakes at twilight: I stepped in, didn't think
to see if you had followed, silence
pulling, shimmering, down corridors, through
walls. But when at last I turned and called, the echo
told me.
        Like the moonlight
drifting in those never-furnished rooms.

The Art of Fugue

I

A room, a table, and four chairs.
The chairs are made of wood,
the floor is wood,
the walls are bare. But windowed.
West light, east light. And a scent
like cedar in the air. Here, the self
will sit down with the self.
Now it will say
what it has to say. It looks
into its own eyes. Listens.

II

A table, four chairs, east light,
west. This is your self:
what's left
when it has been forgiven
by itself, when it
forgives. You feel it — it's
the weight of breath,
transparent, clear.
It folds its hands,
looks up at you. You listen.

III

The self. They've told you
that there's no such thing. A truth.
But one of many. Come
from the other side, from underneath

erasure, chew your way through light toward
different intelligence: you find
that something, even in the task of letting go,
goes on, has been; and in the cold shock of the plunge,
your feet touch bottom. Sound
comes out of silence, is
its inner sense. The river of your
listening, and the river of your voice.

IV

West light, east light, a wooden table
and four chairs: multiple, multiple, multiple
are the voices of the inmost heart.
Sister, brother, husband, wife.
Father, mother, daughter, son.
The compass points of human being
and the being of red alder and
the black-tailed deer. Sleep and hunger,
hope and loss. Silence,
and the bar of sunlight on the floor.

V

Sleep and hunger.
Hope and loss.
Sister, brother,
mother, son.
The floorboards of the soul
are birth, are death,
the four-eyed love
that makes a child.
The patterns in your life
repeat themselves

as premonitions, sudden gifts.
A scent like cedar
drifting in the room. A table
and four chairs.

VI

Once again, the moment of impossible
transition, the bow, its silent voice
above the string. Let us say
the story goes like this. Let us say
you could start anywhere.
Let us say you took your splintered being
by the hand, and led it
to the centre of a room: starlight
through the floorboards of the soul.
The patterns of your life
repeat themselves until you listen.
Forgive this. Say now
what you have to say.

VII

The dead are dead:
parents, siblings, children, spouse.
Death comes upon us:
blindness, deafness, madness, or
the slow gag of neglect.
Put your arms around them:
they are what is given, as you knew.
Hand takes hand.
Dave Dravecky: cancer of the elbow.
Sigmund Freud: cancer of the mouth.
The man who had a heart attack,

and who survived,
because he fell in love.
Your own death, lifting from your past
to meet you: palmprints multiple and
shaped to match your own.

VIII

So it begins. Silence
gathers, looks up, and becomes
a voice: the thrum, the distillate,
we call a soul. Impossible
translation, for the breath
that moves in you
is wind, the wind
that cherishes the trees and cools
the stars. You are,
you are not,
nothing, shaped
by what you love. The echo
of what's left when everything
has been let go.

IX

A voice from the other side, a river: here,
the current steady, there, thickened with silt —
shoals, sandbars, the spill of grief, misunderstanding,
hope and love. You've come
to it before, birdwatching maybe,
looking mostly at the trees. But
now you know. Now you will set
the suitcase down, the backpack, and the book

you love, the book you haven't read, your lunch.
The water's neither cold nor warm.
Your mind has never been as clear.

     X

Once again, the moment of impossible
translation: how good it is
the heart has settled out its load
of wanting and regret. To take
what's left and lead it to the centre of the room —
a table, four chairs, and the river
of the human voice. The floorboards
have been swept, the room
is bare, square to the compass of
your death and birth. You fold
your hands, look up — it's
nothing: light
ahead of you —

Schumann: *Fantasie*, Op. 17

Everything already lost: this always
is the moment where we must begin.
Ecstasy: the self's ghost
standing where you left it, paralyzed,
aghast, and joy, praise,
flooding your lips, your fingertips, the voice in you
huge and exquisite, its mouth
on the nape of your neck.

The west light, the north storm,
to have known, not to have known:
because that touch was silence
and the body is your home,

you will be named,
you will be seen,
the wing will open in you,
breaking. You,
caught in the slipstream of
your own bright anonymity,
you will be spoken to,
stunned, helpless, the wave rising through you
in the dark. Don't
pull the curtain: let the black pane
see you: you,
in the mouth of the night.

Not knowing, knowing:
each worse, each holding
decades in its hand: kitchens,
dumb jokes, kindness and the shine
on the knob of the gearshift in the February sun.
If there were a sword, a block, you think
you'd lay your head along that coolness,

close your eyes. But no,
the blood springs elsewhere, touch
flooding you with silence. You are born
and born again into your life.

If I were able, love,
to be with you eternally, if all things were
already lost. *Take then*
these songs I sang you,
north light, darkness, home, the ache
of the invisible and the pine trees
resinous with sunlight in the afternoon. O, the silence
in that naming, breaking
as you listened. And where the god stood inside you,
an empty shape, a wing.

Note: The italicized lines in this poem are translations of lines from Beethoven's song cycle *An die ferne Geliebte*, Op. 98, on which Schumann based melodic material in the *Fantasie*. The original German texts are by Alois Jeitteles.

Autobiography

In the years when winter snow piled up
along the edges of the streets, beneath the windows,
on the lee side of the hedge,
I did my homework at a desk my father built,
set in the corner of my bedroom, facing west.
Which was my choice, I think. The second desk,
I know it was. And once I moved out, the apartments
with the bad floors and the crazy plumbing,
the wallpaper I was always steaming off, I'd take
the place because it had a workspace
that did not face east.

Those cold bright years.
How long I spent, trying to die.

Such injustice. When every morning
it's spring again. Every morning
the light melts the snow —
before books, before desks, before windows,
before pain, before amazement.

Autumn Again

for Don McKay

Late August at my window: the restlessness
in the dying grass, no longer drawn by light
but only air, the light itself — unflexed,
the fluid stretch of summer done —
moving inside itself, unseeing.
                                        All day
the crickets chanting, bright glitter on the surface
of the ebb. And ravens
talking to themselves, the flocks
of chickadees. What is
human happiness? Last night, the broad leaves
of the grass at dusk fell still, the stillness
falling through them, breathing out
its heft of dew. I stood a long time at the window
listening: crickets in the darkness,
chanting, chanting.

An Abridgement of a Conversation with Jan Zwicky

Warren Heiti: You have written that "it's a matter of justice and respect to let poems speak for themselves." One reason — which you provide via Northrop Frye — is that poems are not made but midwifed. Another reason (which I lift from elsewhere in your work) is that form is internally related to content: "how you say is what you mean." My worry is that the very gesture of agreeing to talk *about* the poems, in a discourse that is *formally* different from them, already constitutes some kind of betrayal. Wouldn't it be *much* better for us to attend a concert of Bach's music, or to go for a hike and look for nuthatches?

Jan Zwicky: The focus of this exercise is supposed to be my poetry. But I can't talk in a meditative way about my own poems. For one thing, I'm mostly critical of them. I could complain at length: there are so many ways in which they fail to capture the shape, the perception — I don't know what to call it — "that wordless configuration in the world which lit up, which arrested my attention." But such complaining — in public, anyway — is both bad manners and deeply uninteresting.

Then there's the fact that it seems graceless to talk about one's own work. Is the poem an "achievement"? This is a tricky question. P.K. Page, in keeping with many other poets, said that the poem spoke itself through her — that she was a kind of conduit for something whose origin was "outside" her. If the poem is a kind of oracle, however, then it might seem that no credit devolves to the poet. But this isn't quite true. Writing a poem is not unlike catching a fly ball. You mustn't think about it — if you do, you'll muff it. But if you don't think, if you just run to exactly the right place and leap in exactly the right way at exactly the right time, there it (sometimes) is in your glove. Some poets have made absolutely spectacular catches; but I would be loath to stand up in public and say, "Did you see that?" about a catch I myself might have made. This attitude may be incomprehensible to the Facebook generation, which has been brought up to believe that it *must* advertise itself. And there may indeed be something generational in my response. There may also be something gendered — Virginia Woolf writes in *A Room of One's Own* that anonymity "runs in [women's] blood." But I think that the wish to remain anonymous with respect to one's own writing goes deeper than either culture or gender because you see it in artists of all genders across a great range of societies, proclivities, and talents. Its root is the intuition that lyric insight occurs only when the "self" isn't blocking the view. To remain true to the insight, however poorly one has rendered it, the "self" has to stay out of the way. If the testimony of poets themselves isn't enough, Iain McGilchrist in *The Master and His Emissary* provides neuropsychological evidence that this is the case.

Finally, there's the problem of talking about the work at all. Suppose one of you were to say something like, "Enjambing here throws the weight on this noun, and that's a surprise. Did you mean to pick up on the image in the second line?" My honest answer will often be something like, "I didn't intend anything. I just searched and searched until I found something that felt right. I tried that line break and suddenly the gesture the words were making was a little more in tune with the wordless shape that was haunting me."

Well! So now I've gone on for three paragraphs about what I don't want to talk about. Apologies!

Darren Bifford: I'm curious about the fly ball analogy. This is certainly a sentiment shared by heaps of creative thinkers in all fields. Yet don't you think there is a danger here for this analogy in the literary field? Doesn't it lend itself to ideas of Romantic inspiration? (Not in itself wrong; inspiration is a real experience.) Suppose we invoke an alternative analogy, that of a craftsperson, and considerations of technique that go with it? I think about the drafts of W.B. Yeats's "The Second Coming," for example. Seamus Heaney remarks that for Yeats the poetic act "is not one of complaisance but of control.... Where we can think of Wordsworth going into a trance, mesmerized by the sound of his own voice, we have to think of Yeats testing and trying out different voices and deciding on which will come most resonantly from the mask.... Yeats does not listen in but acts out. The origin of the poetry is not a matter of sinking in but of coming up against, the mature music is not a lulling but an alerting strain." Do you think this is coherent with the intuitions you've described above?

JZ: I'm not certain that technique makes one *available* to lyric insight — either as a reader or a writer. (Both depend on the same skill set.) For me, and for others with whom I've worked as an editor, it seems that technique gives you the strength to make something of your availability. But the availability is a separate matter. A poet can be available, can see the ball, correctly sense the speed and trajectory, and yet not have enough muscle to catch it — can't leap high enough, or crouch low enough, or twist the glove just so. And there are also folks with loads of technique who aren't that available, to whom no breathtaking balls have been hit. Or who at least seem not to have seen anything really worth catching.

Although I think there's a distinction between the fly ball of insight and the mechanics of craft, this doesn't mean there isn't work for English teachers to do. First and foremost, they can read great poems aloud. This is the single most important way of convincing potential readers there really are lyric fly balls and that some people have actually caught them. And then there's the history of literary endeavour in whatever language is being read; and grammar; and vocabulary; and what used to be called rhetoric and dialectic — facts (yes! facts!) about diction, prosody, logic, argumentation, sentence and paragraph structure. One can't begin to read literature if one has little command of the language in which one reads, nor a sense of its possibilities of style. Command of this sort is to reading what core strength is to physical balance. And if you want to improve your balance, you don't get up in the morning and focus exclusively on the act of balancing. You get down there on the mat and build up your abs. Similarly, if you want to learn to read with discrimination, sensitivity, and insight, you first work on the basics: how to write a simple grammatical sentence; how to write a complex grammatical sentence; how to phrase a question politely; how to phrase it in a challenging tone; the rules governing acceptable combinations of nouns, verbs, adjectives, and adverbs; how to punctuate for grammar, and how to punctuate for rhetorical effect.

And what about the other aspect of lyric literary art — the "availability" I mentioned? Charles Simic describes it as an eye for the similar and the significant. But he's mystified by its occurrence, and it's clear that he could just as well be talking about inspiration. It might be dangerous to talk about inspiration if we mean by it some kind of metaphysical hocus-pocus with invisible other-worldly beings who toss lyric baseballs at their favourite outfielders. But if we mean what Simic does — that most of the time poets, like everybody else, stare at the world in incomprehension; and that occasionally they don't, that occasionally, for reasons we don't understand, poets and other lyric artists are suddenly available to the connexions — the real, significant similarities — that are actually there in the world all the time — then, no, I don't think it's dangerous to talk about inspiration. It might even be important to talk about it. What's dangerous is to imagine that human beings can *invent* truth. For poetry — the real thing — is indeed true.

Darren, you suggest that a better analogue for the poet than the outfielder is the craftsperson. I don't see that there's a difference. Both have technique, and both have to place that technique in the service of the real if their activity is going to inspire — to stir up availability in — the rest of us. If a potter is going to make a pot worth having, she has to have a lyric eye as well as good hands and a strong back. It's wrong to suggest Wordsworth was mesmerized by the sound of his own voice if we mean by that that he was not devoted to craft — look at

sions to *The Prelude*. Wordsworth did, however, "listen in" more and
~~ss~~ than Yeats. But it's Yeats, I think, who was more captivated by the
~~his~~ own voice, and with the idea of himself as a maker. And look what
~~to~~: "The Circus Animals' Desertion." *Players and painted stage took all my*
love ~~and~~ *not those things that they were emblems of.* If I had to choose between
never writing another poem and feeling that I'd failed to attend to reality, I'd
choose never to write another poem *in an instant.*

What is it like to be available? For me, some being, some action, some scrap
of memory, some musical phrase — an emotional/visual/aural/kinaesthetic/
intellectual/*perceptual* complex "in an instant of time" — will stand a little
forward in the world, will be haloed with visual or aural light, and suddenly I
will have a feeling of terrible responsibility toward it, as though I need to *do*
something — to honour it, to pray in gratitude, to offer due acknowledge-
ment. Usually this pressure is wordless and I feel utterly inadequate to the task
of cherishing — nothing I could do could possibly be enough. Would I be
happier in a culture that encouraged people in such moments simply to fall
on their knees? I often think so; but then I realize that's not quite right,
because Simic is also right: there's also pressure to see or to hear *properly,* to
perceive all the connexions and to perceive them justly. Writing the poem can
help one do that. It's as though the image-complex, the one that's standing out
a little (and I must stress that for me the image-complex is often predomi-
nantly aural), has a tail that you can sense disappearing under the baseboard.
You have to feel your way along that tail, stretch and squeeze your soul's arm
under that baseboard and find out where the tail goes. Because what the
image-complex *means* is another image-complex to which the tail is *tied*; and
it means *that* it is tied and *how* it is tied. It has been said that Pablo Neruda's
genius consisted in his capacity to *stay under* so long. This sounds right.
Staying under is staying with the haloed being or situation; you don't want to
breathe because you might jostle it. It takes great strength of non-mind.

Ah, Darren, it's just struck me. Maybe what you're pointing to in trying to
get us to focus on craft is the way we register meaning in our *bodies*? You're
thinking that if we focus on the *body* of the poem, we'll get to the place of our
own deepest response?

DB: Yes. That's one way of thinking about this. But I didn't intend to suggest
that the analogy of the craftsperson is *better* than that of the outfielder
catching — at the limits of her or his reach and ability — a fly ball. They're
complementary. In fact the analogy to which I've often returned is that of
the musical improvisation: how a lifetime of practice and technical mastery
is necessary — though not sufficient — for the possibility of improvisation,

which for jazz musicians is the most perfect expression of their art. And this turns out to be very close to Aristotle's vision of *aretē* in *Nicomachean Ethics*.

JZ: The analogue of the jazz musician is superb! The outfielder, the craftsperson, as honed improviser. Free because disciplined. The observation applies to classical musicians who are good sight readers, too — especially folks who get together to read chamber music. Well: it applies to anyone who is a good reader of anything. *It's the same skill set.*

Tuesdays, before my yoga class, a dance class meets in the same space. They're rehearsing for a musical in a few weeks. We're a small, remote community, so it's a motley crew. The instructor clearly has experience but most of the dancers, equally clearly, have almost none. But there was this one girl … The music was bumptious, the lyrics skanky — a 1920s nightclub act. And she'd found these moves — not even the instructor had them. When she stepped forward ("left!"), then back ("right!"), there was a swing that wasn't just in her hips; it was in her ankles, in the balls of her feet. At the climax, the dancers were supposed adopt a profiled pose and to extend their right arms along their right legs and shake their hands, fingers splayed, like a tambourine — you've seen the gesture, right? Only, this girl raised her shoulder a bit first, then thrust her wrist down her leg fast, in a slightly scooped motion, the whole hand bent back before she did the tambourine thing — it was rhythmic, raunchy, and just a tad elegant; utterly captivating. And I'll swear she wasn't aware of doing it, wasn't thinking — she didn't move like a pro, nor did she seem self-conscious. Her dancing had organic form: she'd made herself available to the music, and, respecting the syntax of the choreography, the music was inhabiting her body, expressing itself *through* her body.

That can happen with poetry, too. Poetry has organic form when the music of being inhabits the body of someone's language, when the gesture of speaking becomes *physical material, stuff,* that the music can express itself through. A poet's voice is what corresponds to the dancer's body. The music of being doesn't express itself through "language"; it expresses itself through *someone's* language. This is mysterious: what we refer to so casually as "voice" — meaning something like linguistic compositional style — is, in fact, the poet's (that is: the poet-as-poet's not merely the poet-as-human-being's) *body.* Voice is *as* unique, *as* physical, and *as* <u>informed</u> by imagination as the body of the dancer, the body of the jazz musician, or the body of the athlete. It's hard to wrap one's head around. We're so used to thinking of language as something abstract. I mean, here it is, right now, on the page — "disembodied," we might say. And isn't this disembodiment the genius of writing? (That we use fantastically abstracted glyphs to notate thinking-and-feeling, and send these glyphs over great distances to other humans, who then can *read our thoughts* without our physical presence — no hands, no faces, no mouths, no vocal chords.)

Yet the arrangement of those glyphs is *inflected* in exactly the way the body is inflected by music when it dances. Voice is physical — although because our culture is literate, we can distinguish an apparently disembodied aspect. But it can't be anything more than an aspect — something that shows up when we light the whole just so — and it can't really be distinct. (Or, better, it can be distinct but not separate.)

When we're composing, then, we search kinaesthetically — as Dennis Lee says. And as readers we also search and stumble until our body finds the way. Organic prosody and what we call voice are one phenomenon: a poet placing the body of language-as-it-is-first-genetically-manifest-in-her-or-him-and-then-disciplined-by-education,-experience,-and-conscious-effort in the service of the music of being. I've done poorly with that hyphenated string (although I puzzled over it long enough). It seems to me that we've discovered a huge gap in Western European, perhaps literate, philosophical vocabulary.

What's "organic prosody"? Denise Levertov didn't exactly write the book on it, but she did write an essay: "Some Notes on Organic Form." It's a superb piece. One thing she points to, without using the word, is Max Wertheimer's notion of *Gestalt*: a whole, which we discern first, and which determines the natures and dispositions of what can then be discerned as its parts. Her essay concludes with the ecstatic image of this *Gestalt* sustaining us as we leap from image to apparently discontinuous image.

This "apparent discontinuity" is important. It is, in some sense, merely apparent because the *Gestalt* does comprehend the whole. And yet the gaps cannot be filled in with words. The words that make up an achieved lyric poem *are all the words there are*. To spell things out more explicitly would be like explaining a joke: it would shut down the auditor's or reader's capacity to make the connexions for her- or himself. Actively making those connexions is the point of the exercise: to *experience* the shock of insight, as the poet did, not be *told* about it. T.S. Eliot says in "East Coker" that poetry is a raid on the inarticulate. I don't think that's true. I think poetry is a raid on the *articulate*. We don't go out hunting with our linguistic bows and arrows and try to bring down a lyric insight or two. Instead, it's as Warren, explicating Woolf, says elsewhere: insight wells up through the debris of syntax and reference and *captures* them — a gyre, or a vortex, or, let's let the liquid metaphor go, the *Gestalt*'s gravity starts to affect language the way a magnet affects iron filings. (Sometimes, in some contexts, the filings line up nice and straight; other times, they pile and clog and cluster — both testifying to the presence of the field.) The poem comes from outside language. That is, lyric insight does not have linguistic form — it takes language by surprise. Voice reflects the trace in language of the gravitational field of the haloed object *through* the poet's body.

That's the difference, and one of the reasons it's hard to think about this stuff. The obvious metaphor of the field makes it look like the action of the haloed object on language has to be direct: in physics, fields can occur in vacuums. But *this* field, the lyric field, behaves like sound: insight requires a medium for its transmission. That medium is the individual — in the sense of the particular and individual*ized*, the unique and uniquely inflecting — *body* of the poet.

WH: Let me circle back to touch on two things you've mentioned. First, your response to the question "What is it like to be available?" I share your feeling of terrible responsibility; and I feel throttled by sorrow over my own inadequacy to meet that responsibility. ——— But are our responses apt? (And here I am only reminding you of something you have asked me in the past.) Shift the focus just a little, and we see that it could be different: instead of fixating on the lack of beauty in ourselves, focus on the beautiful: isn't that an occasion for *rejoicing*?

The second remark I want to return to is your suggestion that the image-complex has a tail. I agree: *sometimes* it's like that. But sometimes, I think, it isn't. What I mean is more clearly expressed by the two aspects of *nature* that you distinguish in "Lyric Realism." Under one aspect, an image-complex is a set of relations (it has a tail). But under another aspect, it is *this particular thing* "that stands out, haloed, against the chaotic backdrop of 'everything else.'" (The two aspects have their correlates in the distinction that Robert Hass tries to draw between metaphor ("this is that") and image ("this is")). But the emphasis on internal relations in "Imagination and the Good Life" makes me wonder whether the first experience (image-complex with a tail) is paradigmatic for you.———

JZ: As I was struggling to find words for my experience of the image as a beast with a tail, I was thinking all the while about Hass's distinction between metaphor and image, a distinction that, when I encountered it, produced an immediate and involuntary salute. What you say is important, accurate, and just. But, no, most of my experience of availability is indeed simply of image-complexes — individual things, or situations, or events — standing out against their backdrops. Invariably, though, if I can stay under long enough, I sense — well, *more*. And it's not until I sense that *more*, until its shape, too, begins to be discernible — that's not quite right: — : until my availability is stretched to extend to it, too (although that's also not quite right: it's often more like achieving sufficient interior darkness for some dimmer trace to register — nothing so active as stretching) — anyway, it's only then that the haloed image-complex — the "individual" thing, situation or event — stands *stably* in my perception.

It's when I sense the shape of the *more* that I can *bear* it.

Yes, also: grief. I've been talking about this experience as though it were all in a day's work, when frequently it is unbearable.

But focusing on its unbearability is, in a way, ridiculous. It's as you say: we need to be able to shift the focus a little. A few people I have known have been good at this shift. All of them have had a serious spiritual or meditative practice. I believe it's because they *accept* their inadequacy, their inability to bear the awe, that they are happy. They are able to see that their inadequacy is just a fact, like the leaflessness of the winter aspens or the muddiness of the dugout — just how it is with us humans. This wisdom allows them to have compassion for the self. It's that compassion that shifts the focus and gives sustained access to joy.

Selected readings

Eliot, T.S. "East Coker." *Four Quartets*. London: Faber and Faber, 1959. 21–32.

Frye, Northrop. "The Archetypes of Literature," §VII of "My Credo: A Symposium of Critics." *Kenyon Review* 13.1 (Winter 1951): 92–110.

Hass, Robert. "Images." *Twentieth Century Pleasures: Prose on Poetry*. New York: Ecco Press, 1997. 269–308.

Heaney, Seamus. "The Makings of a Music: Reflections on Wordsworth and Yeats." *Preoccupations: Selected Prose 1968–1978*. New York: Farrar, Straus and Giroux, 1980. 61–78.

Lee, Dennis. "Body Music." *Thinking and Singing: Poetry and the Practice of Philosophy*. Ed. Tim Lilburn. Toronto: Cormorant Books, 2002. 19–58.

Levertov, Denise. "Some Notes on Organic Form." *Poetry* 106.6 (September 1965): 420–25. Reprinted in *The Poet in the World*. New York: New Directions, 1973. 7–13.

McGilchrist, Iain. *The Master and His Emissary: The Divided Brain and the Making of the Western World*. New Haven, CT: Yale University Press, 2010.

Page, P.K. "A Writer's Life." *The Filled Pen: Selected Non-fiction*. Ed. Zailig Pollock. Toronto: University of Toronto Press: 2007. 3–22. Published online in 2005.

Simic, Charles. "Narrative of the Image: A Correspondence with Charles Simic." With Charles Wright. In Charles Wright, *Quarter Notes: Improvisations and Interviews*. Ann Arbor: University of Michigan Press, 1995. 57–74.

Woolf, Virginia. *A Room of One's Own*. Harmondsworth: Penguin Books, 1965.

Zwicky, Jan. "Imagination and the Good Life." *Common Knowledge* 20.1 (Winter 2014): 28–45.

———. "Lyric Realism: Nature Poetry, Silence, and Ontology." *Malahat Review* 165 (December 2008): 85–91.

———. "What Is Lyric Philosophy?" *Common Knowledge* 20.1 (2013): 14–27.

Acknowledgements

The editors would like to thank Bethany Hindmarsh, Amanda Jernigan, and Robbie Moser as well as the copyright holders who granted permission to reprint the following poems.

The New Room (Toronto: Coach House Press, 1989)

> "Practising Bach"
> "Language Is Hands"
> "Leaving Home" I, II, & VIII
> "The Horse Pull"
> "Your Body"

Songs for Relinquishing the Earth (London, ON: Brick Books, 1998)

> "K. 219, Adagio"
> "The Geology of Norway"
> "Brahms' Clarinet Quintet in B Minor, Op. 115"
> "Cashion Bridge"
> "Bill Evans: 'Here's That Rainy Day'"
> "Beethoven: Op. 95"
> "Driving Northwest"

Robinson's Crossing (London, ON: Brick Books, 2004)

> "Prairie"
> "Epistemology"
> "One Version"
> "Robinson's Crossing"
> "History"
> "Another Version"
> "Glenn Gould: Bach's 'Italian' Concerto, BWV 971"

Thirty-seven Small Songs & Thirteen Silences (Kentville, NS: Gaspereau Press, 2005)

> "Small song in praise of ears"
> "Small song for the voice of the nuthatch"

"Small song: Prairie"
"Small song to oneself"
"Small song: Mozart"
"Small song: Laundry"

Forge (Kentville, NS: Gaspereau Press, 2011)

"Music and Silence: Seven Variations" I, IV–V, VII
"Late Schubert"
"Practising Bach"
"Gemini"
"If There Were Two Rivers"
"From Distant Lands"
"The Art of Fugue"
"Schumann: *Fantasie*, Op. 17"
"Autobiography"
"Autumn Again"

lps Books in the Laurier Poetry Series

Published by Wilfrid Laurier University Press